English Business Meetings Phrase Book

Alan François

1st Edition

Copyright © 2024 Alan François

This is dedicated to my teacher who wanted me to become a best-selling author,

while I ended up as a teacher instead.

About the author

Raised in East London, awarded a scholarship to attend City of London School, graduated at Westminster, then taught at The College of Haringey, Enfield and North East London before moving to France to teach and coach high level managers and directors in Paris in various sectors including Pharma, Media, Aerospace, Real Estate and Legal. With over ten years of experience bridging the culture gap in negotiation styles through various dynamics, always reflecting on the impact of body language, performance and trending negotiation techniques, he brings these uniquely intertwined insights to his work at Sorbonne University, ESLSCA Business School, Metropolitan Formations and this book.

Table of Contents

Introduction

1. Organising the meeting
2. Opening a Meeting
3. Negotiations

3.1 Starting Position

3.2 Getting opinions

3.3 Rejecting / Disagreeing

3.4 Reaching a compromise

3.5 Closing the deal

4. Ending the meeting

Introduction

Welcome to the BLUE edition. There are many nuances in any language, so if you want to know about the meanings and when to use each phrase, it's recommended to get the RED edition, which explains the theory and contains exercises to help you improve.

Just to recap, in English, here are some points to consider before picking a phrase:

1. Be sure of your relationship before using informal and direct English.
2. Use emotional and grand adjectives to have an impact.
3. Show awareness and present a benefit to motivate the receiver.
4. To be more polite and formal, use a longer sentence.

1. Organising the meeting

    a. Asking
    b. Availability
    c. Changes
    d. Roles
    e. Common Phrases

Asking

Whether on a call or in an email, the opening formula is still the same:

[Greeting] + [Ask about health] + [Reason for meeting]

Informal / direct

- Hi X (optionally: how are you?), I need...
- Can you give me a time to meet?
- Hi, what's up? Can we meet Friday?
- 'Ello, you good? I need to have a meeting with you!
- Hey, let's meet on ...?
- Hi, can we meet on ...?
- Hiya, how you doing? Need to meet about *x*. When's good?
- I'm trying to book a slot with you, how about ...?
- Can we find a time for a meeting next week?
- Alright, let's pencil a meeting for Tuesday at *x*.

Formal

- Hello X, I hope you are doing well. Would it be possible for us to have a meeting in May?
- We need to meet about x, when would be a good time for you?
- Let me know if that isn't convenient.
- Can I arrange a meeting with you next week?
- I'm calling to see if it's possible to reserve a meeting this week?
- Is it possible to book a meeting with you between 3 and 5pm?
- It would be great to meet to discuss this. Do you have any availability next x?
- I would be happy if we could meet next week! Please give me your availability.
- I would be pleased to meet you on …
- I would appreciate the opportunity to present our solution for your project. Is there a chance the team could meet you on …?
- Is there a time we could all meet together to…?
- Good morning, Mr/Ms/Mrs X, this is *Y* from *Z*, how are you today? Great, I'm calling about the email you sent, when would be a good time to have a meeting or call? Now? Ok, great…

- Hello Mr/Ms/Mrs X, I hope this reaches you well. Would it be possible to have a meeting with you to discuss y? For example, I am available on *x* day, between *x* and *y*.
- The project booking is a little complicated, can I send you the dates or would you prefer to have a meeting?
- Here are the dates, I'm sure it looks complicated, I understand if you need to have a meeting about it.
- Here are the dates, please let me know if there is a problem, thanks in advance!
- Here are the dates, I hope there won't be a problem. Kind regards,
- Here are the dates, all booked. Best regards,

Directive/Formal

- Hello X, I have scheduled a meeting for 4pm.
- Dear Team, I will hold a meeting on *x* at *x* and will be delighted to welcome you.
- Dear Team, the meeting is scheduled for *x* on *x*, and I would be delighted if you can attend.
- Regarding your proposal, **I am available Wednesdays after 1pm. I would prefer a call rather than a physical meeting**, thanks.

Reservations

- Hello, I would like to book an appointment with X, please.
- I'd like to reserve the meeting room for an hour at 2pm, please.
- My bathroom seems to be clogged. Can I book *X* as soon as possible please?

Availability

Checking the agenda

- Can you give me a minute / second?
- Could you give me a minute please?
- (Could you) Let me check my agenda...
- One moment please...
- Just (for) a moment, please...

Rejecting

- (informal) I'm busy
- I'm afraid I don't have any availability
- I'm really busy right now, could you call back later?
- I'm sorry that week is completely full.
- I'm totally booked up for the month, I'm afraid.
- I'm fully booked that day, I'm afraid

Proposing alternatives

- Let's say next week!
- Can we say next week?
- We could meet at...
- How about...
- Well, I will be available from 2pm to 5pm
- That seems good, now, we believe we would need to increase the meeting by 30 minutes, if that's alright with you.
- Well, I have a meeting for 3 hours just before that time, I would need a little break!
- I'll be away until the end of March, so perhaps it would be better if...

Accepting

- I am available on….
- Well, I have an opening at…
- (informal) I'm free on…
- Ok great, see you at 6pm!
- Right, I'll see you in two days, looking forward to it.
- Yes, we'll be attending / participating on Monday, looking forward to it!

Persuading

- Ok, I understand you're busy, now I would just like to know the timeframe and whether there a deadline?
- I see, now I understand we might have to stay later, start earlier, or have lunch, as your business is very important to me. How about…
- We have an opening in the production schedule, I'm afraid it's either that or a much longer wait.
- Would you like to reschedule a call for next month? Well, I'll be away next month, which could cause you significant delays, if we don't get this off the ground now.
- Do you need this project to start quicker, or can we hold off? I don't mind, but you do understand

that I can't guarantee availability further down the line.
- Alright, now I would just like to know how much revenue can you afford to lose?

Reasons for changes

- Unfortunately...
- I'm afraid I have to...
- Due to reasons beyond my/our control, we have to ...
- Due to reasons beyond control, it is necessary to ...
- My colleague double booked the room!
- It's no longer possible for me to attend.
- I'm afraid we've had a setback!
- I have / there is:
  - an urgency/ emergency.
  - an urgent matter to attend to.
  - a personal issue / problem.
  - a family matter/emergency to deal with.
- I've had to accept a medical appointment at short notice.
- There's a company emergency.
- I've had some difficulties with the transport...
- Something urgent has come up.
- There is a conflict in my agenda, sadly, it seems it will be difficult to maintain our meeting.
- My train won't arrive before 4pm, so can we delay the meeting by 10 minutes?
- Well, I'll say yes, but I hope we can wrap up by 5pm, I'll need to catch a train.
- I seem to have a connection issue, can we delay the meeting for a few minutes, please?

Requesting a later meeting time

- Please accept our apologies but it seems we will need to postpone.
- Could we push the meeting back?
- I'm afraid we need to put off the meeting for a short while.
- Is it possible to put back the meeting?

Requesting an earlier meeting

- ➢ A slot has been freed up, we could advance the meeting time, if you are available.
- ➢ Is it possible to bring the meeting forward?
- ➢ Could we push forward the meeting?

When you have no preference

- ➢ X sends his apologies, but would it be possible to move our meeting?
- ➢ I was wondering if we could reschedule?
- ➢ Due to the transport issues, we feel/believe it's better to rearrange our meeting. We hope Xth is suitable for you, if not, please reach out to us on +xx xxx xxxx to re-align our availabilities.
- ➢ We've been confronted by some logistical hurdles that are impossible to overcome at this point in time. We've reorganised our schedules with a target to meet in *x* on the following dates, between *x* and xx am. Please confirm at your earliest convenience.

2. Opening the meeting

   a. Starting
   b. Welcoming
   c. Apologies
   d. Objective
   e. Agenda
   f. Timing
   g. Modifications
   h. Moving between items

Starting

- Let's get down to business.
- OK, shall we make a start?
- Right, let's go!
- Now, it's xx:xx, so let's get going with our meeting.
- Well, ladies and gentlemen, time is pressing, so we will have to make a start.
- Alright, now that everyone's here, let's start.
- Right, as we have a lot on the agenda, it's time to begin.
- So, without much further ado, let's begin.
- Alright, good day everyone, it's a little after xx:xx, so we had better get started.
- We've had a request for a late start, due to *x* being stuck in traffic, so please help yourself to tea and coffee, as we will start in 15 minutes.
- Alright, I'd like to call the meeting of *x* to order.

Welcoming and introducing

- Welcome, everybody.
- I'd like to start by welcoming everybody.
- I'm happy to see everyone!
- What a great turnout here today!
- Thanks for attending/ being here/ on time
- Firstly, I'd like to introduce…
- Let's go around the table and introduce ourselves!
- Shall we go around the table?
- Roll call!
- Today, we have in attendance our valued shareholders, to whom we'd all like to offer a warm welcome.
- Our wonderful interns are present to take the minutes, which will be forwarded to you shortly after the end.

Apologies for absence

- I'm afraid that *x* cannot be with us today because…
- We/I have (received) apologies (for absence) from…
- X sends his/her/their apologies.
- Unfortunately, *x* is missing today…
- I would like to offer my apologies for ….
- Sadly, it's not possible for *x* to attend today…

Objective

- Our objective/aim/goal today is to…
- Today's objective is to….
- We have *x* objectives…
- I've called this meeting to look at the question of…
- We need to cover *x* and *y*…
- I'd like to talk about the ideas put forward in the feedback from last month's survey.
- In today's meeting we will discuss the proposals and how we could create new leads for…
- As you know from the agenda, we need to decide…
- We need to make a decision.
- We need to take a decision.
- We have several choices and need to select…
- We are meeting to establish the…
- We're called together to finalise the terms of our contract and continue the great relationship between *x* and *y company*.
- Today's meeting will clarify the figures of our agreement with *x company*.
- By the end of our meeting, we will have defined the core strategies to put in place to achieve our desired targets for this year.

- The objective of today's meeting is to precise which training we need to supply to our workforce and which company to employ.
- Simply put, our objective is to revise our CSR approach, and we will explain why this is crucial for the company.
- We have received a bid, and we are here to discuss the benefits and drawbacks.
- As an emergency, we have an audit tomorrow and we need to explain these figures.
- X has launched a takeover bid, so I've gathered our legal team with the board to recommend our next steps.

Introducing the agenda

- Now, the agenda/ plan/ order of the day has *x* items…
- Have you all seen a copy of the agenda?
- Can we take it as read?
- We can assume everyone has seen the agenda and the minutes from the last meeting, so…
- OK. As you can see from/on/in the agenda, there are *x* items.
- Firstly… secondly… thirdly… finally…
- Can we start with… then come on to… and finish with…?
- As you know in the agenda, we will look at…
- Is there any other business?

Timing

- Today's meeting will last an hour.
- We have *x* minutes, so I would like to spend *x* minutes on a, then *x* on b, ….
- Item *x* will start at xx am and finish at xx:xx.
- I hope our meeting will last *x* minutes / take no longer than *x* minutes.
- We are scheduled to finish at / by *x* p.m.
- I will / would like to speak for about…minutes.
- I plan to speak for about…minutes.

Modifications to the agenda

- Can I bring / draw your attention to point/item *x*?
- Unfortunately, it seems there is an issue with item *x* so we'll postpone/table it for now
- As Jon isn't here, we're skipping item *x*.
- Item 4 has been moved up the agenda as it is urgent.
- We've brought forward item *x*.
- Can we bump this one? It doesn't seem so important.
- In the order, item *x* has been swapped with item *y*.
- In relation with/ to item 2, I should tell you that…
- Regarding the new appointment of…
- Concerning the proposal, we have an update…
- With respect to item 5, we have a slight modification…
- As a matter of urgency, we have a new item, which is…

Example:

Right, if I could have your attention, please, thank you, now it's a little after eleven, I think it's best if we get started. *X* will probably join us in a few moments, I'm sure *Y* can bring *X* up to speed, right, *Y*? Good, so let's get down to business. Today's meeting is about ABC, and our objective is to finalise our decision on which offer to go with. We have about forty minutes and as you know from the agenda we sent out, three presentations from X, Y and Z, after which we need to settle on which bid to accept. As X is running late, we'll skip that and start with Y. Are there any questions? Alright, let's proceed with the first part, Y, if you may…

Moving between items

- Let's / let me / I will / we will begin with…
- Let's start with…
- Beginning / to begin with (x point), let me explain…
- Let me start by outlining the advantages of…
- Now let's talk about…
- The xth point is…
- Now that we've covered x let's move onto y.
- That covers everything with x so let's go to the next point which is y.
- I think that clears up everything with x so can we move on to y?
- Let's move on to point x.
- Moving onto point x.
- Moving on, let's look at item x.
- The next point is….
- That brings / takes us to the end of this point
- To sum up / summarise ….
- That summarises the point about x
- This proves
- Right, that's all I wanted to say about…
- OK, I think that covers everything on…
- I think that deals with…
- To end this point,
- To finish before we move on to …
- To close this point

- Now that's done, let's move to
- moving on
- let's move on to
- continuing on
- This brings / takes / leads me to my next point, which is…
- I'd now like to move to the next point which is….
- Let's move to…
- Moving on, let's ….
- The x point is…
- (Now) let's now look at…
- Now I want to turn to…
- Let's move along to…
- This brings me to the third and final point which is…

3. Negotiations

- Starting Position
- Probing Interests
- Making an offer
- Opinions
- Rejecting / Disagreeing
- Reaching a compromise
- Agreeing
- Nibbling
- Renegotiating
- Finalising

3.1 Starting Position

➤ So, thanks again for inviting us today, and we really appreciate it, now I think we have a proposal that you'll like and lead us to a win-win.

➤ Here's the situation:

➤ Here's the proposal:

➤ Here's what we need:

➤ Thanks again for coming today, now here's what we are looking for: …

➤ As we discussed over the online meeting, we both want to close this deal, there are just some finer details to iron out.

➤ We are very interested in your proposal now there are a few things we'd like clarified.

- Right, so let's get down to the nitty gritty, we need *x* and we're prepared to pay *x*.
- Just to clarify, this is just a preparatory meeting, whatever we agree on still has to be ratified by direction.
- Let's not beat around the bush, we would like to offer you *x*.
- Simply put, the price is too high, but we're interested to meet you halfway.
- Ladies and Gentlemen, here is the new price for the year, I'm here to answer any questions you may have.
- Considering item *x*, I have a few thoughts I'd like to share…
- I'd like to draw your attention to…
- One of the most important aspects of this is…
- The key point here is…
- What we want to do is acquire your business, so we'd like to hear your terms, we're all eyes and ears!
- We're looking to strike up a partnership with you and place our product on your channel, sound good?
- We would like to enter into a contract with you for a period of *x* years for the sum of *x*, how does that sound?

- We've been very impressed with the performance and would like to extend the contract, albeit with a few changes/stipulations.
- After the presentation, we were certainly persuaded to sign, but we have a few conditions.
- As you are aware, we put out a call for tender, and you responded with an interesting bid, now we just want to examine some areas in closer detail, as with the approaching election, the proposed timeframe is now rather precarious.
- We really like x, and while the price is reasonable, we would like to propose some concessions in certain areas so we can fit this into our budget.
- Our companies want x and y, so we're here to discuss how to do that.
- We only have this one opportunity to finalise a deal, or my client is walking/going elsewhere. Let's do our best, ladies and gentlemen.
- As you all know, we have a presence in every country, every store, and we'd like to bring your product into our family. You may find a better price, but you simply will not find a better partner.
- We're looking for a partner and your bid was impressive. However, the price is simply not within our interests. We have three areas where we believe we could streamline and make the proposal more cost effective.

- So, you know we have some concerns with the proposal so we're willing to entertain any ideas to make this a profitable outcome for us both.
- Right then, let's dive in. If I understand correctly, you've seen some interesting offers from the competition and would like to see if there is any possibility of us matching them, is that right? Let me explain…
- As you're aware, we have had to make some heart-rending decisions to streamline the company, so this is your opportunity to share any ideas and give feedback, as this affects all of our futures. The first action on the business plan is to…
- So here we have our target for this year, it might seem challenging, but I wanted this meeting to discuss with you a new position and the responsibilities that go with it, I assume you're interested?

Creating rapport

- I know how you feel,
- I know nobody wants to be here so early so I'm going to make this as quick as possible
- If we want to get this done, we need to work together to...
- We don't need to spend time on this.
- I know what you are/were thinking.
- I'm sure everyone in this room...

Probing Interests

- Is this a bad time for a meeting?
- So, what did you have in mind?
- What does your company actually need?
- What do you think you require to make this meeting a success?
- How can we improve this business?
- We need *x*. How would this affect you?
- What would be the impact for you?
- After this deal, what's your project for the future?
- Please bear in mind, we're looking to lay the groundwork for working together in the future.
- How can we establish a longer-term partnership?
- What does your manager expect?
- Are you planning to expand into that market? Perhaps we could help, as we have a foothold via *x*.
- Well, if you (can) scratch my back, I will, of course, scratch yours.
- We will, of course, reciprocate any efforts made to make this a win-win.
- What are your priorities?
- Let me make sure I understand your perspective.

Acknowledging

- I'm sure you don't need me to tell you that...
- I realise you all know...
- To be clear, when we talk about *that*, it isn't about you personally, it's simply a business proposal, we like working with you and are happy to review any feedback you may have.

Softening with diplomacy

- I tend to think that...
- It seems to me that...
- That may be a little/bit difficult.

Rhetorical questions

- How will this affect our company? I think it's clear that...
- What will be the result? Well, I think the result will be...
- How can we explain this? Let me show you...
- Is there anything we can do about this? The answer is...
- Why should you agree? We provide...
- Why should you go with us? Well, ...

Giving background

- As we know,
- As you know from this morning's news, we...
- Per the last reported figures, we have...
- As published today,
- According to the balance at end of closing,
- If we consider the size of the most recent bid,
- Referring back to X,
- As we saw in X,
- As far as I know,
- As far as I understand,
- Data shows that X is ... which leads us to conclude that "statement XX" is true / accurate.
- Data proves that...
- X is evidenced by the (study/ data/ etc).
- We can see that X is better (etc) due to the data described here (pointing at slideshow).
- Did you know that...?
- According to a recent study...
- I read (in x source) that...
- Statistics show that...

Making an offer

- Here's our opening offer, of course we're open to negotiation.
- Ok, here's our offer:
- After listening to your needs, here's our initial proposal:
- Alright, all things considered, we are prepared to offer you the following:
- Thank you, ladies and gentlemen, for all your points. So, here's the offer:
- After some discussion, here's what we've got:
- We've taken into account the points you raised, so I hope you will appreciate the offer of:
- Well, I think you'll be happy with the following:
- Upon consideration, we've made some alterations and can offer you as such:
- So, considering your proposal of an extended contract over five years with the inclusion of site visits and priority client support, we hope you will be prepared to accept x million, which would be paid over those five years in annual instalments, which we think is reasonable.
- Alright, great, so let's summarise, you'll supply x hundred thousand items, take care of logistics and delivery to our y stores, by x of April. In the case of late delivery, you agree to pay x in

damages, meanwhile we'll pay by x January via bank-to-bank transfer, in euros. If the payment is late, we agree to pay 4% in damages. This agreement covers two years. If everything is in order, we are ready to sign.

- ➢ So, we agree that the bond will be underwritten by x of London, with a maturity date of 10 years, with the caveat of an early call back with the penalty clause of 1% of the current sum, unaffected by interest and/or inflation.

3.2 Getting opinions

- How do you feel about…?
- What do you think (about this)?
- What's your view (on this)?
- Why don't you share your view?
- What's your take (on this)?
- How do you/we feel about …?
- What is your feeling on this?
- What are your feelings about this?
- Do you have any questions?
- What's your view?
- Are we agreed?
- Would you like to comment?
- Any remarks?
- What did you think about?
- What's your opinion about my presentation?
- How did you feel about …?

Eliciting opinions

- Would you like to say something?
- You look like you want to say something
- (to associate) Can I bring you in here?
- (Perhaps) we could hear from you/x?
- Let's hear what x has to say (on the matter/subject).
- We haven't heard from you yet, x.
- Can we hear what x has to say?
- Can we listen to what x has to say?
- x, you look like you want to say something
- x, would you like to say something / comment / add something?

Giving opinions

- In my /our opinion….
- I / we think
- I believe
- In my opinion
- If I were you…
- I would say…
- I can say that…
- I'm of the opinion that
- If I understand well…

Confident opinions

- It goes without saying that…
- Obviously….
- Of course, …
- It's my conviction that
- It's my belief that
- I strongly believe that

Personal opinions

- I think ...
- I feel....
- I believe...
- Well, personally I think
- In my own opinion
- In my own view
- For me, that is...
- From how I see it
- From my/ our point of view... (In / on my point of view is NOT CORRECT)
- From where I'm standing, it looks like
- As far as I'm concerned
- As I take it
- As far as I know
- As far as I can see

Focusing

- I'd like to emphasise the importance of...
- I'd like to stress we need to...
- I should reiterate/repeat, if we don't...
- It is critical/essential to understand that...

3.3 Rejecting / Disagreeing

Rejecting

- I'm afraid that doesn't seem likely.
- I don't think that's feasible, unfortunately.
- That's beyond our scope, sadly.
- That's not something we can really agree to.
- Well, that's as far as we can go.
- In consequence, the share prices would plummet, and nobody wants that.
- You're going to have to take it or leave it, I'm afraid.
- What? But how are we supposed to do that?

Responses to extreme or final offers:

- Let's be reasonable. I think we could go with…
- Please tell me that was a high/lowball.
- What market research is that based on, exactly?
- We've done our research. Unless you have data to back that up, let's not embarrass ourselves, please.
- You're funny! Now, back to serious business, what was your offer?
- And we should accept that because you're the only supplier in the market and we're desperate?

I think you've misjudged the situation. Let's go back a step.
- I'll pretend I didn't hear that.
- That's simply not going to happen.
- Sorry, but we can't do that.
- Sorry, but that would be a (big) 'No' from us.
- You're pulling my leg!
- Are you pulling my leg?
- Are you being serious, right now?
- Well, (*lots of exaggerated breathing noises through mouth, nose and teeth*), I don't think that's going to work.
- Nice try, but we can't possibly accept that.
- You've got to be kidding me.
- (laughing) well I commend the attempt, but we simply can't entertain that.
- If I accepted these terms, come the morning, you'd find me six feet under.
- Well, I'm afraid we've hit a wall.
- Looks like we have a stalemate, that's a pity.
- I disagree.
- I have to disagree.
- I'm afraid I disagree.
- I'm afraid I have to disagree.
- I'm not sure that's possible.
- I'm sorry that's not possible.
- That's not possible.
- That's just not possible!

- That's out of the question!!
- That's absolutely out of the question!!!
- No.

To interrupt

- Sorry to interrupt you …
- Excuse me,
- Can I tell you …?
- Sorry, I didn't hear what you said
- Can I just ask (a question)?
- Excuse me, may I interrupt?
- Can I come in here?
- Could I just comment on that?
- Sorry, what? We never said…
- Hold on a minute! That's not what we agreed on!
- Sorry but we're running low on time / out of time.
- - so, could we come back to this later?
- – could we (briefly) summarise the most important point(s)?

When interrupted

- Sorry / Excuse me but:
- I would like to...
- May I finish
- Can I finish
- Could I just finish please?
- Could I carry on?
- Could you please let me continue?
- If you could (just) let me finish...
- If I could finish what I was saying...

Tagging out

- Let me bring in x, who can explain this in more detail
- X, can I bring you in here? As the person responsible for our budget, you can shine a light on the issue for our client.
- X, I know you have a lot of experience. Could you comment?
- Perhaps, I can ask *X* to answer that question? *X*?

Tagging in

- If you could allow me to come in here...
- Sorry, may I interject?
- Allow me a moment to explain, after all, I'm in charge of that.

Bad cop

- What are you doing?
- Are you kidding? Do you know who we are?
- Do you even realise the chance you have to get this meeting? Don't waste our time.
- Are you trying to ruin us?
- There's no chance.
- (To good cop) What are you doing? (Almost whispering) We're supposed to close this deal at 55k!
- Please let me negotiate the offer, (looking at good cop) you're too soft.
- You do realise your position, don't you? We can walk away at any time, it's you who needs our business, we can go elsewhere.
- *Use all the rejection phrases in anger*
- I'm not sure what you're expecting but we're not going to yield over this.
- Are you kidding me? There's no way.
- I hope you're aware that we hold the upper hand here.
- What was that? Did you get that from a YouTube video? This is real life, that's not going to work here.

Good cop

- Let's keep things amicable, shall we?
- I think it's in both our interests to find a reasonable outcome.
- Would you mind if we have a quick word privately, I have some new updates on our position.
- Sorry but he's going through a difficult time, he's a bit liable to explode so let's try to avoid mentioning the price for the moment, he's under a lot of pressure to hit a target, so you know, he definitely wants this deal.
- I've just received a message about the price, just need to jump on a call, won't be more than 5 minutes!
- Well, we might be able to help you there.
- Look, I like you/your approach/company, don't worry, I'll take care of *bad cop*, but I'll need your help to calm him/her down. Don't you have some wriggle room in your margin?
- Let's remember why we're here, it's not personal, we've all got to make a profit somewhere, that's business, we just need to find the right conditions for a win-win.
- Let's not poke the bear here, it's likely to storm off.
- Let's keep things amicable, shall we?

- I think it's in both our interests to find a reasonable outcome.
- Would you mind if we have a quick word privately, I have some new updates on the situation.
- Sorry but he's going through a difficult time, he's a bit liable to explode so let's try to avoid mentioning the price for the moment, he's under a lot of pressure to hit a target; just so you know, he definitely wants this deal.
- I've just received a message about the price, just need to jump on a call, won't be more than 5 minutes!
- Well, we might be able to help you there.
- Things seem to be getting a little heated, how about we take a little break?
- Look, I like you/your approach/company, don't worry, I'll take care of *bad cop*, but I'll need your help to calm him/her down. Don't you have some wriggle room in your margin?
- Let's remember why we're here, it's not personal, we've all got to make a profit somewhere, that's business, we just need to work together to find the right conditions for a win-win.
- Let's not kill the golden goose, we have a good thing going here.

3.4 Reaching a compromise

Confirming comprehension

- If I understand correctly,
- If I follow correctly,
- I'm not sure I follow, do you mean…
- Are you saying that…?
- Are you implying that…?
- What I understand is, we will…
- From what I understand, we will
- From my understanding,
- To summarise,
- (informal) You get me?
- (informal) Yeah, I got you!
- I'm not sure I get what you mean…
- (informal) Did you get what I mean?

Responding positively

- That's a good / difficult / complex / an interesting question.
- Thank you for asking that question.
- I'm glad somebody asked that question. It allows me to say...
- I accept that.
- That's a fair point.
- I agree with what you're saying, more or less.
- Up to a point, I agree.
- You're being very generous! However, ...
- Well, there's something you haven't considered...

Not taking a position

- That may/might be true
- That could work
- Maybe
- Perhaps
- Possibly
- Potentially

Partly Agreeing

- I see what you mean but/however
- I know what you mean
- I hear what you're saying
- That's an interesting point but why don't we consider …
- Right, however there must be room for a reduction.
- Right, but surely there's room for a reduction?
- Right, and surely there's room for a reduction!
- Right, now surely there's room for a reduction?
- I understand what you need but I'm not sure we understand how we can do that. How do you imagine us doing that?

Position driving

- Very good, now we require *x* and *y*.
- I think the best way forward would simply be to accept our terms.
- That's a good / nice idea, however we're more interested in...
- Our partners/shareholders wouldn't accept that notion.
- We are prepared to give you x. I have the authority to say there's not much else to say about it.
- Thanks for coming, now we only have a small window to make this happen. You need to find a way to bring the price down or some way to streamline your offer or something else to add to the offer or the client will simply not be satisfied. We're listening, go.
- We're not looking for that, can you provide this?
- I'm afraid there's not really any room for negotiation.
- ... And that's the bottom line.
- Do you need to call your superior? If they could see what they could gain, I think they would agree. Let's expediate the process, we all want to move forward on this, can you call them now?

Acknowledging

- Yes, I see.
- I understand what you're saying.
- I see what you're getting at.
- I know what you mean.
- So, you mean that...
- So, if I understand correctly, you want....
- You seem to really need that.
- I can see that's really important to you.
- I see you really care about your employees/ product/ clients.
- I see why they say that about you.

Handling difficult questions

- I'm afraid I'm not really the right person to answer that. Perhaps...
- That's not really my area/field, I'm afraid. You could ask...
- Sorry, I don't have the figures with me, but I will...
- I'm afraid that question goes beyond the subject of today's meeting. I'd be glad to discuss that with you personally afterwards.

Tennis

- Well, let me ask you the same question.
- OK. Let me ask you a question.
- I can deal with that by asking you a question.

Hedging

- Well, that depends on what you mean by…
- Well, that's a very complicated matter…
- Well, there are various ways of looking at it…

Suggesting

- I think you /we should / could …
- By the way, I suggest (less direct)
- (can) I suggest (more direct)
- Could/ May I suggest…
- If I were you, I would…
- It would be good if we could
- Can we…? / Could we…?
- I suggest that we…
- My suggestion is that we…
- I recommend that we…
- My recommendation is that we…
- I propose that we…
- My proposal is that we…

- What about…?
- Why don't we …?
- Maybe we could…
- How about…?
- Could I propose…?
- Isn't it time we …?
- I think it's about time we…
- We'd better do this because my boss is going to eat me alive.
- Let's figure something out quick, can you crunch those numbers again?
- It would be in our best interests to come to an agreement before 5pm.
- Can't we just agree to that? I'd love to celebrate at the bar with you, let's go, let's go!

Questioning

- Why don't we...
- Have we considered...
- How about...
- Can we...
- Could we...
- May I...
- Have you seen/heard/ ...
- Put yourself in my shoes, how could I make that happen?
- How can I do that?
- How are we supposed to do that?
- Are you against the idea of...?
- How can we make this work? I'm sure we both want the same outcome.
- Would that work?
- How would that work?
- How can we achieve a mutually beneficial outcome?

Redirection / decoys

- We can't really budge on this price. (*Later on*) Alright, we'll make an exception, just this time.
- It's very important to know that our priority is to sell this at (x price).
- Just so we're clear, that price can't really move.
- I'm not *really* comfortable with discussing the price of x, but perhaps if things go *really* well, well, let's come back to this after the other points.
- Let's look at the market price… Is this really much better?
- Show us the cheapest in the range… now do you really want to sell that to us?
- Do you know another party with a better offer?
- Take a look at this…
- Well, if we compare with the competition, we cannot be beaten.
- You're more than welcome to research, you'll find we are very competitive in terms of quality-price ratio.
- The leader in this market is X, but with our new strategy, we are in a strong position to challenge, and it can only be beneficial to create partnerships now, isn't it?

Supporting with a previous point

- Going back to what John was saying
- As we were saying
- To go/get/come back to what I was / we were saying
- Could we continue with x, as we said, it would be better if…

Presenting solutions with "what"

- What we can't do is…
- What I'd like to do is…
- What is really important is…

Repeating twice

- This is a very, very difficult problem.
- We thought for a long, long time about this.
- We need to do something, and we need to do it now.

Simplifying

- To be honest…/Frankly speaking…
- Basically…/To put it simply…
- Believe me…

Stressing key words

- We **did** achieve many things last year.
- It **does** seem to be the best solution.
- We **did** think very carefully about this.
- I agree, it **is** important.
- We have tried **repeatedly**, believe me.
- There is **a lot** of room for improvement.
- There **is** a lot of room for improvement.

Using dramatic language

- A total/absolute/complete disaster!!!
- A great/outstanding/remarkable success!!
- Completely/ totally unacceptable!
- Absolutely/Quite brilliant!
- Astounding / surprising results!
- Fantastic / Incredible!
- It is risky → It is commercial suicide.
- This may be a problem → This will lead to chaos.
- We need this → This is an absolute must.
- Some will complain → There will be a riot.

Contrasting for effect

- Actually…/In fact…/In reality…/The truth is that…
- Yesterday it was easy. Today it is far more difficult.

Adding ideas

- In addition to this…/Moreover…
- However, …
- Despite this…
- So…/Therefore…/ Consequently

Checking understanding

- Are there any questions or comments on that?
- Would anyone like to raise / ask a question at this point?
- X, did that answer the question you had about...?

Explaining advantages

- The main advantage/disadvantage of this is....
- I think there are two main reasons why this is far superior to/ better than...
- So, if we did this now, rather than in *x* months, wouldn't you gain *y*?
- It's clear: if you do this, you will get that.
- Clients usually see a x% uptake in sales within x months. Would you like to see the data?
- You will have a clear advantage, you do see that, right?

Three times

- This new product is faster, cheaper and more efficient.
- This supplier is friendly, customer-focused and next door!

Bargaining / compromising

- Well, if you could do *x* then we could do *y*.
- If you can propose *x* then we would be more open to doing *y*.
- We could do *x*, on the condition that...
- Now we can't do that, however, if we can find a way to do *x*, then it's a done deal.
- We would be more comfortable with...
- If we give you *x*, could you lower *y*?
- Would you be willing to do *x*, if we do *y*?
- How about if we give you I? Would that work?
- That's not going to happen. Unless...
- Tell you what, we could do *x*, if you can do *y*.
- Help me to help you! What if you...
- I'm not sure the potentials are clear, here. We have a customer base of *x*. Compared to *y*, you stand to gain *z*...
- What if we simply split the difference?
- We need to reach a consensus here, why not...

- I'm trying to envisage how we can move forward amicably... how about...
- I see you feel strongly about this, so if we agree to that, can you find something to sweeten the deal?
- Look, I have to go back to my boss with something. I mean, would you go back empty handed?
- How about if we extend the terms of the contract for a longer period, which means prices are locked in?
- You know one of our clients paid for all this and gave us a five-year contract, while you're asking for the same at two-thirds the cost, which we may be able to do, but only because my manager has a good relationship with yours, but the outcome of this deal could change all that in the future. Do you want to take that risk and be responsible? Are you sure this is your bottom line?
- Ok look, we're prepared to take a loss here, because we need your business, as long as you extend the contract.
- Ok, you win, we can't afford to waste time over this. Let's sign.

Persuasion

- We appreciate your efforts, really, it's noted. Other suppliers have been *shaking head*, so we especially want to make this happen, and to work together in the future. So how about...
- I like the way you worked with us, now...
- I can see you're a good person, I want to keep working with you.
- You're good at this, how long have you been x?
- We want everyone to be happy, right?
- I like the way you do business, X.
- That would make me so happy, X.
- You're going to make a lot of people happy.
- It's not just money, is it? Think about the good we can do.
- When the department hears about this, they'll be cheering your name.
- We will remember what you did to make this happen, X, and we will thank you for it.
- Think about the difference this will make to their families.
- People need this, we can make this happen.
- You're going to make your people proud.
- You wouldn't want to make them unhappy, would you?
- You know what's best, make the call.
- Well, that wasn't hard, was it? Now how about...

- We already agreed to do x, so adding y won't really make a difference, will it?
- Ok, now, I'm doing you a favour here.
- We don't have much of that left, but I can keep the rest of it for you, right now.
- What do you think would be the best outcome?
- What do you think will happen to x if we agree to do y?
- I know you think x is going to happen, now what about if we do y? Wouldn't that work?
- You know, we tried this before, and it didn't work out- turnover increased by 28% percent. Do you want to risk that happening with you?

Ultimatums

- We need to come to an agreement; time is running out.
- We have to do that, unless you want this deal to go south?
- Thank you for your offer, now I could get the same thing from our current supplier. Is there a way to reduce the price? If not, well, thank you for your time.
- Your offer is very interesting, but we are not in a position to pay that price range at this time.
- Either we…, or…
- If we don't…, then we will see…
- This is a must, otherwise…
- We have no choice but to do…
- I'm afraid that's the best we can do.
- We need to understand the facts, we have to sell.
- We need to accept facts, there isn't any other way.
- Do you want us to walk away and tell everyone what happened here today?
- Ultimately, if there's nothing that can be done, we will have to walk away and that will certainly be a pity.
- Well, that's our final offer, take it or leave it.

Agreeing

- Yes.
- Alright!
- Right on!
- I agree.
- Good!
- That's true.
- You're/That's right.
- You're/That's correct.
- I agree with you.
- I can agree with/to that.
- Ok, I suppose I could agree to that.
- We can do that.
- I am agreed.
- We are agreed.
- Let's do that, then!
- That's true.
- (yes) I (do/ totally) share your point of view.
- Exactly.
- You're (perfectly/ etc) right.
- Precisely.
- That's a great idea!
- I'm all for that!
- Sure!
- Fine!
- Great!
- I'm (totally) with you (there)

- Great!
- Excellent!
- Brilliant!
- Absolutely!
- Wonderful!

3.5 Closing the deal

- Ladies and Gentlemen, we have a deal.
- Looks like we have a deal, nice work, everybody!
- So, to sum up, …, are we agreed? Fantastic!
- That's a deal! Thank you so much!
- Wonderful, thank you, good doing business with you.
- We're going to make a lot of people happy.
- Thank you, no, the pleasure was (all) mine, great deal!

Nibbling

- So, that's a done deal, fantastic. Just, one more thing...
- Ah we didn't mention the delivery cost, can you take care of that?
- Oh, I forgot to ask about the bank charges for the currency conversion, can you bear those? It won't really make that much of a difference, will it?
- Ok let's sign! Now there are just a couple of minor things to finalise but I'm confident we can do that over the phone tomorrow.

- Ah, what about x, let me throw that in, I'll discount that too.
- Wait a minute, we didn't mention X, now that would be great, can we have that as well?
- By the way, we can also offer you *XYZ*, right now at a discount.
- That's not in the contract so can you email me to that effect?
- Can I get that in writing, obviously we trust you, but just in case we forget; we're only human.
- Can we just add the cost of the *x*?
- Would it be a problem to get this notarised?
- Oh, there's a public holiday so the bank will be closed tomorrow, can you expedite the payment, so it arrives today? Then we can get the ball rolling, as it were, without further delay.
- By the way, do you mind footing the bill for the x? It's no big deal for you, is it?
- How about we tack on another two months? You know, sweeten the deal even more, considering the concessions we made, we're good, right?
- I'm assuming you're hosting our travel costs? I'll email the flight receipts to your assistant.

Renegotiating

- I'm afraid there's been a setback, we didn't discuss the cost of x. We need to go back to the table.
- I thought we had an agreement, but there are some extra costs that were not made clear to us. We need another meeting or the deal is off.
- I ran the proposal by the CEO now there are some further details we need to pin down.
- I'm sure you're aware, we're within the cooldown period and we've had some new developments that will affect our agreement.
- We had a great negotiation, and we still want to work together, but there are some things that we've noticed that simply cannot work. Let's please have a meeting about this, or do you want to throw away the progress that we made?

4. Ending the meeting

1. Questions?
2. Summarise / Conclude
3. Thanks
4. Organise next meeting
5. Goodbyes

Questions
- Does anyone have any questions?
- Any questions?
- Would anyone like to ask a question?

Summarising
- So, we covered…
- We talked about…
- The points today were…
- In summary, …

Concluding
- So, we will…
- So, we have decided to…
- What I understand is, we will…
- From what I understand, we will
- From my understanding,
- To conclude…
- In conclusion…

- To conclude, I'd like to say that…
- I'd like to finish by saying…
- That concludes our meeting about x
- So, our final recommendations are to:
- It seems to me, then, that we should…
- I would therefore recommend/advise that…
- My own proposal would be to…

Mentioning support and follow up

- I have prepared some handouts which I will pass round.
- I'll give you my email address in case you want to follow up something I said.
- Do contact me if you would like more information on this.
- The recording/ presentation file is in the email/ shared document online.
- Feel free to message me if you have any further comments or questions

Organising

- Shall we meet on ….
- Let's reconvene on…
- Let's meet again on…

Thanks

- Thanks for listening
- Thanks for attending
- Thank you so much for being here
- Thanks to *x* for organising the buffet
- I would like to thank *x* and X
- All my thanks to X
- I am grateful for the food / to *x* for the presentation
- I would like to give my thanks to *x* for doing…
- I would like to give *x* my thanks *x* for the …

Goodbyes

- Thank you and goodbye.
- I look forward to seeing you …
- See you next …
- Best wishes for …
- Hope you have a nice/good…
- Good luck with …
- Have a great week.
- Remember it's not 'goodbye', it's 'see you later'!
- It was good to meet you,
- Enjoy the rest of your time in…
- Thanks again for a great meeting, all the best, now!

This is the end of the phrase book! Hope it was useful! If you want to read about the theory behind the phrases, pick up the RED edition! Now go have a great meeting and good luck!

No AI was used to create text, but it was used to create the front cover portraits. You may find a mistake in the text somewhere, after all, I'm only human.

You can find me and other materials at
http://www.orochinagi.com/English

www.ingramcontent.com/pod-product-compliance
Lightning Source LLC
Chambersburg PA
CBHW070357230526
45471CB00006B/2606